HEALTH MATTERS

Allergies

Carol Baldwin

Heinemann Library
Chicago, Illinois

©2003 Reed Educational & Professional Publishing
Published by Heinemann Library,
an imprint of Reed Educational & Professional
Publishing, Chicago, Illinois

Customer Service 888-454-2279

Visit our website at www.heinemannlibrary.com

Designed by Patricia Stevenson
Printed and bound in the United States
by Lake Book Manufacturing

07 06 05 04 03
10 9 8 7 6 5 4 3 2 1

Library of Congress Cataloging-in-Publication Data
Baldwin, Carol, 1943–
    Allergies / Carol Baldwin.
        p. cm. — (Health matters)
Includes bibliographical references and index.
    ISBN 1-40340-247-7
    1. Allergy—Juvenile literature. [1. Allergy.] I. Title.

RC585 .B35 2002
616.97—dc21
                              2001007970

Acknowledgments
The author and publishers are grateful to the
following for permission to reproduce copyright
material:

Cover photograph by Damien Lovegrove/Science
Photo Library/Photo Researchers, Inc.

p. 4 Michael Newman/PhotoEdit/PictureQuest; p. 5
Ariel Skelley/Corbis Stock Market; p. 6 Professor S.
H. E. Kaufman and Dr. J. R. Golecki/Science Photo
Library/Photo Researchers, Inc.; pp. 7, 13 Jack
Ballard/Visuals Unlimited; p. 8 Seth Resnick/Stock
Boston, Inc./PictureQuest; p. 9 Bob Allen/Outside
Images/PictureQuest; p. 10 James King
Holmes/Science Photo Library/Photo Researchers,
Inc.; p. 11 Bob Kramer/Stock Boston, Inc.; p. 12
David Young-Wolff/PhotoEdit/PictureQuest; p. 14
Bob Krist/Corbis; p. 15 Trevor Clifford/Heinemann
Library; p. 16 Charles Gupton/Corbis Stock Market;
p. 17 Tom Stewart/Corbis Stock Market; p. 18
Martyn Chillmaid/Oxford Scientific Films; p. 19
Stephen F. Rose/Rainbow/PictureQuest; p. 20 Jeffry
W. Myers/Stock Boston, Inc.; p. 21 Michael A. Keller
Studios/Corbis Stock Market; p. 22 David Young-
Wolff/PhotoEdit; p. 23 Oliver Meckes/Photo
Researchers, Inc.; p. 24 James Frank/Stock
Connection/PictureQuest; p. 25 Alan D. Carey/Photo
Researchers, Inc.; p. 26 Denis Paquin/AP Wide
World Photos; p. 27L Robert F. Bukaty/AP Wide
World Photos; p. 27R John Bazemore/AP Wide
World Photos

Every effort has been made to contact copyright
holders of any material reproduced in this book.
Any omissions will be rectified in subsequent
printings if notice is given to the publisher.

Some words are shown in bold, **like this.** You can find out what they
mean by looking in the glossary.

Contents

What Is an Allergy?

An allergy is a **condition** that causes a person's body to react badly to something that is harmless to most people. Certain substances, called **allergens,** cause **allergic reactions** in people who have allergies. For many people, the **symptoms** of an allergic reaction may be mild, like sneezing or itchy eyes. For other people, they can be serious, like swelling of the throat or difficulty breathing.

This is because allergic reactions can affect many parts of the body. Here are some examples of common allergic reactions:

◆ runny or stuffy nose, sneezing

◆ swelling of the throat, difficulty breathing

◆ burning, itching, or tingling of the mouth and lips

◆ red, itchy, watering eyes

◆ tight feeling in the chest, coughing

◆ throwing up, diarrhea

◆ skin rash or **hives**

◆ drop in blood pressure

It can be hard to concentrate on schoolwork when allergies are bothering you.

Allergens

A substance that causes an allergic reaction is called an allergen. Allergens get into the body in one of four ways:

While a wool sweater will keep you warm, some people can't wear wool next to their skin because they are allergic to it.

◆ Inhaled: Some allergens are breathed in with air. These include **pollen,** perfume, house dust, **mold spores,** and animal **dander.**

◆ Injected: Some liquid allergens are injected, or put into the body with needles, like a shot. Injected allergens include insect stings and some medicines.

◆ Swallowed: Some allergens are swallowed, such as those in foods and drinks, or in medicines that are taken by mouth.

◆ Contact: Some allergens, such as poison ivy or wool clothing, simply touch the skin.

Hay fever

Hay fever, caused by plant pollen, is the most common allergic reaction. It affects between ten and twenty people out of every hundred in the United States. Symptoms of hay fever include sneezing and a runny nose.

What Causes Allergies?

Your immune system

To understand what causes an **allergic reaction,** you first need to know how your body's **immune system** works.

Your immune system defends your body against germs and helps keep you from getting sick. When unwanted substances, such as germs, get into your body, your immune system goes to work. It quickly recognizes that chemicals on the germs, called **antigens,** are not part of your body. It wants to attack the invaders. Next, special **white blood cells** that are part of your immune system make chemicals called **antibodies.** The antibodies attach themselves to the germs. Once the germs are covered with antibodies, other white blood cells catch and kill the germs.

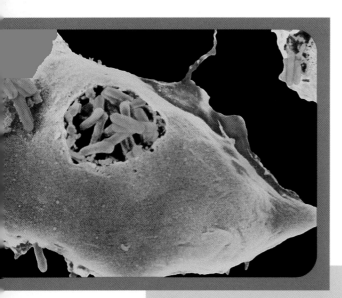

After the battle against the germs is over, some of the antibodies stay in your body. If the same kind of germs invade your body again, your body is able to quickly destroy them because it already has the right kind of antibodies.

White blood cells help you fight illnesses by destroying germs. This picture shows a white blood cell attacking germs.

Allergic reactions

People with allergies have immune systems that are a little too good at their job. Their immune systems don't react only to germs. They also make antibodies against things that aren't harmful to people, like **pollen** or **mold.** In an allergic reaction, a person's body makes too much of a special antibody called **Immunoglobulin E,** or IgE for short.

The release of histamine can cause an itchy rash.

These antibodies attach to cells in the body called **mast cells.** When an **allergen** enters the body of a person with allergies, the allergen attaches to the IgE on the mast cells. The mast cells react by releasing **histamine** and other chemicals. These chemicals are what cause the **symptoms** of an allergic reaction.

Different people can have different reactions to the same allergen. For example, eating peanuts might cause an upset stomach in one person. However, it might cause a rash in another person, and breathing problems in a third.

Who gets allergies?

If you have a friend with allergies, he or she was born with a tendency to have them. This is because some characteristics are passed down from parents to children. Like having red hair or brown eyes, having allergies tends to run in families. A person has a better chance of having allergies if his or her parents or other relatives have them.

People can develop allergies when they are babies, children, teenagers, or adults. Many children eventually outgrow allergies to foods. But other allergies can last a person's whole life. It's important to remember, though, that you can't "catch" an allergy from a person.

Allergies also tend to occur in groups. If a person is allergic to one substance, it is likely that he or she will also be allergic to others.

Children are more likely to have allergies if their parents do. However, they might not be allergic to the same things that their parents are.

Allergic reactions can be dangerous when someone is far from medical aid. People who have allergies should always have their medicine with them.

Serious reactions

Sometimes people have serious **allergic reactions.** Most of these are caused by insect stings or foods. Peanuts and seafood cause the most serious reactions to food. Some medicines can also cause serious reactions. The medicine penicillin, used to treat infections, is the most common one. People don't usually know they are allergic to an insect sting, a food, or a medicine until they have an allergic reaction to it.

Very serious allergic reactions are called **anaphylactic shock.** These reactions can be so bad that people can die. However, this happens very rarely. Most of the time people can treat an allergic reaction before it becomes serious. A medicine called adrenaline can be taken right away to help stop the reaction. Adrenaline is a substance that is made in your body. But when a person has a serious allergic reaction, the body needs more adrenaline than it can make at the time.

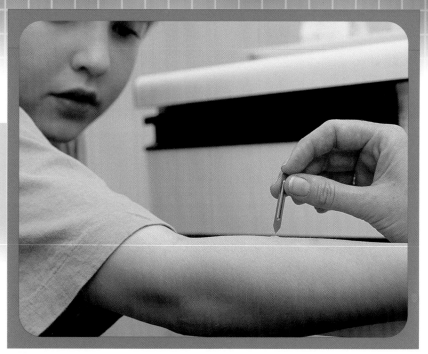

This boy is having skin prick tests to find out what he is allergic to. The tests feel a little uncomfortable, but they don't really hurt.

Diagnosing Allergies

If a person has the **symptoms** of allergies, a doctor will perform some tests to find out if the person has allergies. An **allergist** is a doctor who specializes in treating people with allergies. An allergist uses different tests to find out what substances a person is allergic to.

Skin tests

Two types of skin tests that allergists use are skin prick tests and scratch tests. In a skin prick test, drops of different **allergens** are put onto a person's skin. Then a small needle is used to prick the skin. In scratch tests, the allergist makes several small scratches on the skin. Then a different allergen is rubbed over each scratch.

In both types of tests, the doctor checks the skin around each prick or scratch after about fifteen minutes. If the skin is red, itchy, or has tiny bumps, it means that the person is allergic to the substance that was placed on their skin.

Doctors use a special kind of skin test, called a patch test, to test for allergies to things people touch, such as plants and some metals. They can't use other skin tests for this type of allergen because it may take a day or two for a reaction to occur. In a patch test, patches that contain the allergens are placed on a person's back for two days. After two days, the doctor removes the patches and checks the skin under each patch. If the person is allergic to a substance, their skin will be red, itchy, and bumpy underneath the patch.

Blood tests

Sometimes doctors test a person's blood to see if they have allergies. One test measures the total level of **IgE** in their blood. High levels of IgE show that a person has allergies. Another test measures the amount of certain IgE **antibodies** in a person's blood. For example, if someone has IgE antibodies for peanuts, it shows they are allergic to peanuts.

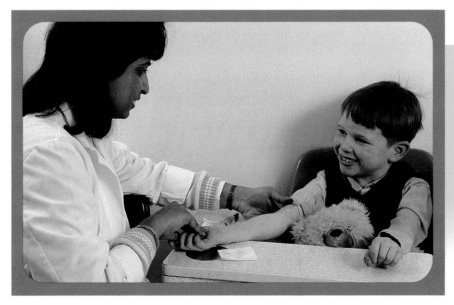

Skin tests usually aren't used for people who have had severe allergic reactions or who have skin rashes on large areas of their bodies. In these cases, blood tests are safer.

Treating Allergies

There is no cure for allergies, but some things can be done to reduce or get rid of the **symptoms** of allergies. The first thing people with allergies can do is to try to avoid the things that they are allergic to.

Avoiding allergens

People with food allergies have to be careful about what they eat. They may find that they can't eat some of the foods they really like. They also have to make sure those **allergens** aren't in packaged foods or foods at restaurants. People who are allergic to **pollen** can avoid it by staying indoors when there's a lot of pollen in the air. People who are allergic to cats or dogs might not be able to have pets in their homes. They may also have to avoid visiting the homes of people who have pets.

Many people with food allergies have to check the ingredients of packaged foods before they eat them. The products may contain tiny amounts of foods they can't eat.

Controlling the symptoms

Sometimes people may not be able to avoid allergens. For example, suppose you have a friend who loves to play soccer or softball. He or she may not want to give up outdoor sports just because they are allergic to pollen. If your friend's allergies aren't too bad, the doctor might suggest an allergy medicine. Allergy medicines help control allergy symptoms. They can be pills, liquids, eye drops, or even nose sprays.

Many allergy medicines are **antihistamines.** These work by stopping the effects of **histamine.** Other medicines stop the body's **mast cells** from releasing histamine altogether. These medicines prevent an **allergic reaction. Decongestants** are medicines that reduce swelling inside the nose. They also help clear a stuffy nose so it's easier to breathe. Other medicines help reduce swelling and **inflammation.** They can be used to treat many allergies.

Some nasal sprays prevent a person's mast cells from releasing histamine. They prevent allergy symptoms from occurring.

13

Allergy shots

Allergy shots can stop people from having **allergic reactions.** They help the body's **immune system** fight **allergens.** Allergy shots contain a small amount of the substance that a person is allergic to. This gets the person's body to start making **antibodies.** These antibodies help block the effects of the allergen the next time a person comes into contact with it. This means that the person's allergy **symptoms** will lessen.

Allergy shots are taken by a certain system. People usually start by getting a shot once or twice a week. When a person first starts the treatment, he or she might get an itchy bump where the shot was given. Putting ice on the area and taking an **antihistamine** will soothe the reaction.

Allergy shots are then given once a week for about six months. After that, they decrease to once every two weeks, then to once a month. Treating a person with allergy shots can take from three to five years.

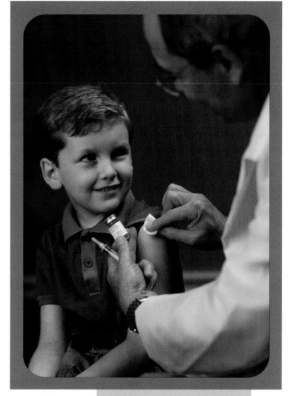

Allergy shots work best against allergies to insect stings and allergens that are breathed in, such as dust, **molds, pollen,** and animal **dander.**

Injection kits

Doctors often give injection kits to people who have very serious allergies. Injection kits contain medicine, usually adrenaline, that people can inject into themselves when they begin having an allergic reaction. The most common type of injection kit is an **auto-injector** because they are very easy to use. Even children can be trained to use auto-injectors.

People with serious allergies must use an auto-injector as soon as they have allergy symptoms. They must keep it with them or nearby at all times. Family members, friends, and teachers should also know how to use the kit so they can help if needed. If you have a friend who has an injection kit, make sure he or she tells you how to use it. A person should go to the hospital after using an injection kit because they might need other medical care.

Most children who need injection kits use auto-injectors because they are so easy to use.

Classmates with Allergies

Food allergies

The most likely place that you will notice a classmate who has allergies will be in the lunchroom. Having food allergies might mean that a friend can't eat many foods served in the school lunchroom. He or she might have to bring a lunch from home. Doing this helps make sure they don't eat something that could cause an **allergic reaction.** You need to be sure not to share your lunch with a friend who has allergies.

Problem foods

A classmate can be allergic to any kind of food, but these are the foods that cause most allergic reactions:

Peanuts

Nuts from trees, such as almonds, pecans, and walnuts

Shellfish, such as shrimp, clams, oysters, crab, and lobster

Cow's milk

Eggs

Wheat

Soybeans

Fish

Children who are allergic to peanuts have to be careful not to eat anything that contains even tiny traces of peanuts.

Classmates with food allergies have to learn a lot about food. You might not know that there is corn in chewing gum and ketchup. You might not know that there is wheat in hot dogs, ice-cream cones, and some candy bars. But classmates with allergies to corn, wheat, or other foods need to learn all the foods they have to avoid. And that's not always easy.

When the pollen count is high, these students don't go outside for recess because they suffer from **hay fever.** Instead, they find other fun things to do in the school library.

Pollen allergies

Some of your classmates might be allergic to **pollen.** Here are a few things that they can do to reduce the amount of pollen they come in contact with:

◆ check weather reports for the daily pollen count

◆ close windows and use an air conditioner when the pollen count is high

◆ stay indoors during the early morning hours, when more pollen is released

◆ stay away from places with a lot of grasses and flowers, such as fields and meadows

◆ stay indoors when grass is being mowed, which can create clouds of pollen

Classroom animals

Does your classroom have animals in it? Many schools have classroom pets, such as hamsters or rabbits. However, some students may be allergic to many animals like dogs, cats, rabbits, hamsters, and even birds. If your classroom has one of these animals, it could make a friend with allergies ill. Your classmates and their parents must be sure to tell the teacher about any animal allergies. Then the teacher can make sure those animals aren't in the classroom.

Your friend might feel bad if the class has to give up its pet because he or she is allergic to it. But, if that's the case, your class could have animals that don't cause reactions in allergic students. Your class could have a fish tank instead, or they might have a snake or a turtle. Hardly anyone is allergic to these animals.

This classroom has a snake because several children are allergic to furry or feathered animals. Many classmates might think a snake is more interesting than other pets.

Insect stings can be very serious for classmates who are allergic to them.

Insect allergies

If you and your classmates enjoy being outdoors during recess in warm weather, chances are you've been bothered by insects, maybe even stung. Most people are a little scared of being stung by insects like wasps and bees, but insect stings are especially dangerous for people who are allergic to them.

An insect injects **venom** into your skin when it stings you. Usually venom is like getting soap in your eyes—it feels painful but does not really hurt you. An insect sting will create a small bump about the size of a pea on your skin. The bump can be itchy and sore and sometimes swollen. For most people, these **symptoms** go away by themselves within a few hours. For some of your classmates, however, insect stings can cause an **allergic reaction** that can be very serious. Their throats might swell and they might have trouble breathing. People who know they are allergic to insect stings should always carry an **auto-injector** with them. They should be able to use it quickly if they are stung.

How You Can Help

Offering food to a classmate who has food allergies could be dangerous for them.

Food focus

Sharing food with friends can be risky if they have food allergies. Unless they know exactly what is in a food, they can't be sure it's safe for them to eat. They might also be embarrassed to tell people that they can't share or trade foods at lunch.

What can you do to help friends who have food allergies? Encourage them to tell others about their allergies, especially if they have serious reactions. That way your friends won't feel pressured to eat something that they shouldn't.

The foods your friend is allergic to can be found in unexpected places, so you should know what to do if your friend has an **allergic reaction.** You should know what medicine your friend takes and where he or she keeps it. You should also tell an adult right away if your friend has a reaction.

Taking care outdoors

Whether or not you have an allergy to insect stings, being stung isn't fun. It can be hard to avoid insects outdoors in warm weather, but here's a list of things that can help keep you and your classmates from being stung:

1. Never drink from a can that has been left open outdoors. Stinging insects are attracted by sugary drinks and may crawl inside a can of soda or juice where you can't see them. The most dangerous place to be stung is in the mouth.

2. Always wear shoes outdoors. Bees often feed on clover in the grass and they will sting if you step on them.

3. Avoid wearing scented perfumes, hairspray, or lotions because they attract stinging insects.

4. Avoid wearing brightly colored clothes, especially those with flower prints. These seem to attract bees and other insects.

5. Food attracts insects, so if you are eating outdoors, keep your food covered as much as possible.

Stinging insects might join you and your friends on the playground in warm weather. Taking precautions can help you avoid being stung.

Visiting a Friend with Allergies

Dust mites at home

Tiny creatures called dust mites live in the dust that builds up in everybody's homes. They live in bedding, carpeting, sofas, and chairs. Dust mites eat tiny bits of skin that people and animals shed. They're so small that they can only be seen through a microscope. Most people don't know dust mites are around because they don't usually cause a problem.

However, dust mite droppings cause allergic reactions in some people. These droppings are very tiny and light. So, when a person flops down on a chair or runs across a carpet, the droppings are stirred up into the air. Many stay floating in the air, and people breathe them in. For a person who is allergic to dust mite droppings, breathing them in might cause them to sneeze and have a runny nose. They might even get a rash or have an **asthma** attack.

One bed can have over 200 million dust mites in it. That's a lot of droppings to cause an allergic reaction.

22

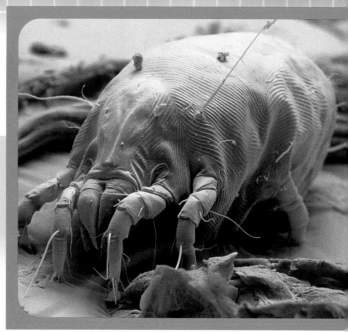

When you look at an enlarged photo of a dust mite, it looks like some kind of ugly monster. In reality, they're so small that you have to use a microscope to see them.

Avoiding dust mites

If you visit a friend who is allergic to dust mites, here are just a few of the things that your friend's family might do to make their home as dust-free as possible:

◆ They use special covers on mattresses, pillows, and quilts to keep dust mites from getting into them.

◆ They open the windows often or use air conditioning because dust mites like warm, stuffy rooms.

◆ They dust surfaces with a damp cloth. This way they don't just brush the dust back into the air.

◆ They vacuum often, using a vacuum cleaner with a special filter.

◆ They choose wood, vinyl, or tile flooring instead of carpeting. If they use rugs, they choose ones that can be washed often.

◆ They wash and dry bedding and rugs at high temperatures to kill the mites.

◆ They also wash stuffed animals often or put them in the freezer overnight to kill the dust mites.

Pet allergies

About seven out of ten homes have one or more pets, usually a cat or a dog. Pets can keep you company and play with you. But many people are allergic to furry animals. Some people also have allergies to horses and farm animals. And some people can be allergic to bird **dander** and feathers. People who are allergic to birds may also react to feathers in down comforters, pillows, sleeping bags, and jackets.

Many people think they're allergic to an animal's fur. But it's actually the **allergens** found in the animal's dander, saliva, and urine that cause allergy **symptoms.** These allergens are often on the fur, but it is not the fur itself. They are very tiny and float in the air. If they get into someone's eyes, they can make them red, sore, and itchy. If they are breathed in, they can make people sneeze, cough, wheeze, and make it hard for them to breathe.

Some people think that animal allergies are caused by long-haired animals only. But, the amount or length of hair on a pet doesn't make it more or less likely to cause allergies.

More people are allergic to cats than they are to dogs. So, some of your friends might be able to have a dog, but not a cat.

Pets at home

Many times people who are allergic to animals still want to have a pet like a cat or a dog. If their allergy isn't too serious, they might take allergy medicines or get allergy shots to lessen the problem so they can have a pet.

If you visit a friend who has a pet they're allergic to, you might notice the following things that the family does to make it easier for your friend:

- They keep pets out of the bedrooms.
- They avoid hugging and kissing pets.
- They wash their hands after touching a pet to help avoid spreading the dander.
- They put plastic covers on furniture where the pet rests or sleeps.
- They wash the pet and its bedding every week.
- A family member without allergies brushes the dog or cat regularly and outdoors. This person also cleans cat litter boxes and bird cages.
- They vacuum often using a special filter in their vacuum cleaner that traps allergens.

Allergy Success Stories

Allergies can sometimes cause a serious condition called **asthma.** People with asthma have sensitive airways. Airways are the breathing tubes that take air from your nose or mouth to your lungs. The airways of people who have asthma are quick to react to anything that irritates them, including **allergens.** Their airways swell up so the space for air to pass through becomes narrower. It then becomes harder for the person to breathe. The person may start coughing, have a tight feeling in their chest, or wheeze. Most people control their asthma by taking medicines.

Doctors discovered that Kurt Grote had asthma related to allergies at the age of two. Because of this, he often had breathing problems. Skin prick tests showed he was allergic to dust mites, **molds, pollen,** and animal **dander.** He took medicines and had a series of allergy shots. At age 15, he started swimming on the advice of his **allergist.** While at

Stanford University, he won five swimming championships. He was also a member of the U.S. Olympic swimming team in 1996.

Jackie Joyner-Kersee is a famous track athlete who has asthma caused by allergies to pollen and foods. She makes sure she takes care of herself and takes her medicines for asthma. She also watches her diet to make sure she avoids foods that she's allergic to. In the 1996 Olympics, she won three gold medals. In one competition, she even wore a dust mask to help filter out pollen.

Former President George Bush is an example of how allergy shots can help a person. He once had a serious **allergic reaction** to a bee sting. Because of this, he had a series of allergy shots to reduce his chances of having another serious reaction to an insect sting. In 1991, he was stung by a bee while he was playing golf. The allergy shots had helped him. Because of them, he only got a small welt where the bee stung him instead of having a serious reaction.

27

Learning More about Allergies

There are many places where you can find out more about the causes, **symptoms,** and treatment of allergies. The groups listed below are just a few. Many websites also offer information about allergies.

Asthma and Allergy Foundation of America
1125 15th Street NW, Suite 502
Washington, D.C. 20005
800-7-ASTHMA

This group studies asthma and allergic reactions to **molds,** animals, drugs, foods, and insect stings. They also offer materials that help teach people about these **conditions.**

The National Institute of Allergy and Infectious Diseases (NIAID)
9000 Rockville Pike
Bethesda, MD 20892
301-496-5717

NIAID is part of the National Institutes of Health. This is a branch of the United States Government. It researches ways to prevent, treat, and manage illnesses of the **immune system.**

Food Allergy Network (FAN)
10400 Eaton Place, Suite 107
Fairfax, VA 22030
703-691-3179

The Food Allergy Network is a group that teaches people about food allergies and the dangers of **anaphylactic shock.**

Peanut-safe schools

Children who are allergic to peanuts can have very serious allergic reactions. More than half of the children with peanut allergies have accidentally eaten foods containing peanuts at some time. This usually happens at school. To prevent this, some schools have made a rule that students cannot bring any food that contains peanuts into the school.

However, the Food Allergy Network doesn't think that this is a good idea. They believe that it's more important for allergic children to learn how to deal with their allergies. Instead, they suggest that the school have a "no food or knife, fork, or spoon trading" rule. They also suggest that all teachers and other school employees be trained to use an **auto-injector.**

Glossary

allergen   substance that causes an allergic reaction

allergic reaction   when a person's body reacts badly to a substance that is harmless to most people

allergist   doctor who specializes in treating allergies

anaphylactic shock   serious allergic reaction that requires immediate treatment with medicine

antibody   substance made by white blood cells that helps the body fight germs and allergens

antigen   germ or natural substance that causes the body to produce antibodies

antihistamine   medicine used to treat allergies; it stops the effects of histamine

asthma   narrowing of the airways that causes people to wheeze, cough, or have trouble breathing. Asthma symptoms are often brought on by allergens.

auto-injector   device that easily injects allergy medicine into a person

condition   health problem that a person has for a long time, perhaps for all of his or her life

dander   flakes of dead skin from animals on which their saliva and other fluids can collect

decongestant   medicine used to treat some allergy symptoms that reduces swelling inside the nose

hay fever   allergic reaction caused by pollen with symptoms that include sneezing and a runny nose

histamine   chemical produced by body cells that causes allergic reactions

hive   swollen, itchy bump on the skin caused by an allergic reaction

immune system   parts of the body, including organs and cells, that work together to defend it from infection and fight off sickness

Immunoglobulin E/IgE   special type of antibody produced when a person comes in contact with allergens

inflammation   redness and swelling

mast cell   special cell that binds to IgE antibodies and releases histamine

mold   living thing that grows on rotting plant and animal material

mold spore   tiny particle that molds send into the air to form new molds

pollen   tiny grains of dust that flowers release and that help make new plants

symptom   change in the body that is a sign of a health problem; the effect an illness or condition has on the body

venom   poison injected by a stinging or biting insect

white blood cell   type of blood cell that is part of the body's immune system. Some white blood cells attack germs that enter the body.

More Books to Read

Deane, Peter and Robert Schwartz. *Coping with Allergies*. New York: The Rosen Publishing Group, 1999.

Latta, Sara. *Allergies*. Berkeley Heights, NJ: Enslow Publishers, 1998.

Silverstein, Alvin. *Allergies*. Danbury, Conn.: Franklin Watts, 2000.

Weitzman, Elizabeth. *Let's Talk about Having Allergies*. New York: PowerKids Press, 1997.

Index